doxecology
STUDY GUIDE
with service plans

RESOUND WORSHIP

SONG & HYMN
WRITERS FOUNDATION
Enriching the Song of the Church

First published in 2020 by the Song & Hymn Writers Foundation.

www.resoundworship.org

A catalogue reference for this book is available from the British Library.

ISBN 978-1-5272-6988-0

Illustrations by Iona Campbell.

The Song & Hymn Writers Foundation is a charity registered in England & Wales, no. 1170493.

Foreword

Peter Harris
Co-Founder, A Rocha International

There is a risk that writing about worship at the outset of a book to accompany new songs and hymns will narrow the view of what we mean by worship. To worship is a whole-life endeavour; as Romans 12 has it, 'to offer your bodies as a living sacrifice, holy and pleasing to God—this is your true and proper worship.' Music, that most physical of acts as the air vibrates and breath is drawn, is just one expression of that offering of our bodies. Scripture sees our offering as a sacrifice, and for it to be 'holy and pleasing to God [...] true and proper,' it demands of us a kind of excellence.

However, just as it is all too easy to shrink our worship into confined spaces that we label religious, so it is now a challenging imperative to expand our sung worship in vision and scope. Five hundred years of Western humanism have demanded a focus on us and our personal lives, but God gives his attention and care to his whole creation. That creation itself is now calling out to us just as its creator intended. As we pay attention, we will hear intimations of divine glory. We will also hear what the prophet Hosea tells us is the earth mourning, and what Paul (earlier in his letter to the Romans) hears as creation groaning.

Since the beginning of the contemporary environmental movement there have been narratives which draw heavily, consciously or unconsciously, on biblical ideas. *The Economist* described this re-told story as 'borrowing only half the apocalyptic narrative (ie the downside). There is a Garden of Eden (unspoilt nature), a fall (economic development), the usual moral degeneracy (it's all man's fault), and the pressing sense that the world is enjoying its final days (time is running out: please donate now!). So far, however, the green lobby does not appear to have realised it is missing the standard happy ending. Perhaps, until it does, environmentalism is destined to remain in the political margins. Everyone needs redemption.'[1]

We can only lament that the initial absence of Christian action and worship from the heart of what *The Economist* labelled 'environmentalism' has muffled the message of redemption which is so critical to any engagement with the earth's groaning. Nevertheless, this new collection of music is a wonderful sign of hope that the Church is beginning to understand the scope of the redemption. In Christ, as Colossians 1 has it, 'God is reconciling to himself all things, whether things on earth or things in heaven' and his gospel is 'proclaimed to every creature,' which is a beautiful description of the work of nature conservation.

It is my prayer that the whole Church will lift up these songs to the Creator and so be inspired to be messengers of hope in his world, carrying a new message of practical good news. If we see that as our calling, then we will see the transformation of the places where the Lord has rooted us, as well as of the people who live in them and with whom we share the gift and the groaning of creation.

1 'The End of the World: A Brief History', *The Economist*, December 2004.

Introduction

Joel Payne, Resound Worship

There is no shortage of anthemic praise songs these days. Nor of passionate songs that reflect on the faithful love of God as Father or friend. But, in a world where the environmental message is growing in volume and urgency, there is a distinct paucity of songs that reflect a coherent biblical theology of creation, or of our place as humans within it. Put simply, there are not enough songs that say, 'We love you, God, *and* we love your world.'

If there is a gap, then it matters. One can all too easily assume that worship is all about adoration. That it is essentially an expression of the internal dynamics of relationship. And worship *is* that. But by no means *only* that. The worship of God's people has always been a response to his covenant love, but it has also been an act of remembering his deeds, of lamenting and hoping, of forming and teaching the next generation. One only has to skim the Psalms to see this. What we sing not only becomes an externalised expression but also an internalised truth.

In the contemporary church we absorb much of our theology from worship songs. Those are the words we repeat, with melodies to aid memorisation, and they become ingrained truths. The core of our worship repertoire becomes the core of our theology. The core of our theology becomes the impetus of our activity. And on issues of creation and ecology the substance of our repertoire is thin, to say the least.

So how did we go about it? Having decided to tackle songs on this theme, we began with a working title of 'Eco Songs'. It was quickly pointed out that 'Eco'-anything was a fairly unappealing title, branding a project as geared towards only those with a special interest in environmental issues. We tossed around the words 'doxology' (praise) and 'ecology' (our relationship to our surrounding environment) for a surprisingly long time before finding our way to *Doxecology*![1]

Early attempts were somewhat ham-fisted. We had taken time to study, to research contemporary theology and current thinking around environmental issues. This was extremely valuable but initially led to five-verse epics which spelled out every aspect of the creation narrative, our corporate failures and our prayers for the future. It was as if we had a lot to get off our chests! We're very much in indebted to Peter Harris who counselled us through this early process, steering us towards a more positive message and challenging us to sing not only about the problems, but about our uniquely Christian hope in the face of them. Ultimately these songs would only serve their purpose if the leaders of worship chose to sing them, so it was crucial to strike the right tone.

Aware that this was an issue much bigger than our own writing group, we decided to open up the process and invite contributions from songwriters across the globe. From those submitted, alongside our own compositions, we would whittle them down to the final collection. We were delighted with the response. There was no way we could include all the 150 or so submissions, but each of those songs was now available to a local church, somewhere, to give voice to their worship. The strapline for this search became 'Songs of Creation, Ecology & Christian Hope' and has remained the heart of the project.

About This Study Guide

Walter Brueggemann, in his book *The Message of the Psalms*, divides the Bible's song book into three categories of *orientation*, *disorientation* and *new orientation*. Those of orientation reflect on the great deeds of God and the wonderful world he made and sustains. Those of disorientation reflect a disintegration of this view in the face of suffering, disappointment and doubt, caused by circumstances which a simplistic faith strug-

1 It should be noted that, around a similar time, Debra Rienstra independently coined the word *doxecological* in a blog piece. See 'Psychoterratica: New Words for a New Earth,' *Debra Rienstra* (blog). Posted 30 March 2019, accessed 11 August 2020, (http://debrarienstra.com/psychoterratica-new-words-for-a-new-earth).

gles to comprehend. Then, the psalms of new orientation are those that emerge on the other side, with a renewed and reformed faith that is all the more authentic for the process and speaks hope to others on the journey.[2]

Though not by design, these three categories correspond remarkably well to our *Doxecology* project. Songs of *creation* reflect on the wonder of what God has done and continues to sustain: themes of orientation. Songs of *ecology* reflect on the current crisis and a troubled world, leading to confession, protest and lament: themes of disorientation. Finally, and perhaps most importantly, songs of *hope* speak of our unique perspective under Christ, the guarantee of redemption and restoration in a perfect future which gives context to all the issues of today: themes of new orientation. We have organised this book of studies by grouping songs in three similar categories:

- the Beauty of Creation
- the Cry of Creation
- the Hope of Creation

Like all attempts to categorise, no single song truly conforms to only one, but it has allowed us to shape the studies with a progression of thought. Each study is related to one of the songs—sometimes very closely, sometimes only loosely—and draws on biblical passages to help expand the doxecology concept, helping us to consider how worship and ecology belong together.

We are deeply grateful to those experts, both practitioners and academics, who have generously contributed to the collection. We're sure this variety brings with it not only a greater depth of insight but also a refreshing balance of voices.

How To Use This Book: Studies

We've pitched this book in an attempt to cover several bases. We hope it

2 See Brueggemann, Walter, *The Message of the Psalms: A Theological Commentary* (Minneapolis: Augsburg, 1984), 15-23.

might be equally useful as a devotional for individuals, a guide for small group discussion and as a sermon primer for preachers. Preachers will no doubt want to go much further than the ideas and applications we have had space to provide, but identifying a Bible passage and providing a few key pointers goes a long way towards getting a sermon started.

For individuals and groups, we'd suggest you approach the studies something like this:

- Read through the Bible passage.
- Reflect: what does this passage say about God? Respond in praise.
- Read the text of the chapter.
- Use the questions either for group discussion or your own reflection, perhaps making notes in a journal as you go.
- Respond with prayer appropriate to the theme.
- Finish by listening to, or singing, the song on the page opposite.

How To Use This Book: Service Outlines

The final section of the book is a collection of three service outlines, prepared by our colleagues at engageworship, one for each category. You'll see that, as well as the song suggestions, prayers and links to other resources, we've suggested one of the studies as a basis for preaching in each service, but you could easily swap the others in and out as appropriate.

How To Use This Book: Online Resources

The service outlines include a number of online resources, which can be found gathered in one place (at www.doxecology.org/resources).

Sometimes, a new song pours out in an instant. At other times it is a long journey, from the initial inspiration through hard work and countless revisions, before the final song emerges. This project has, in large part, been the latter. And I can honestly say that for me, and the rest of the Resound Worship team, *Doxecology* has been a deeply valuable journey of discovery, transformation and worship. I pray that it will be for you too.

Part One

The Beauty of Creation

Heaven's voice brings the dawn,
out of chaos is born
new creation
exploding with wonder;
planets spin into space,
earth and sky find their place,
all of nature
awakes to its maker.

You say everything you've made is good:
the sun, the moon,
the stars that shine above.
You say everything you've made is good:
the land, the seas
and all that lives and breathes.

We sing praise to the maker,
to our King, our creator:
praise to Almighty God.
All creation together
singing one hallelujah:
praise to Almighty God.

We are formed from the dust,
with your image in us,
given life by the breath
you are breathing;
called to work and to care,
called to nurture and share;
called to serve you
and walk where you're leading.

Heaven's Voice Brings The Dawn

CHAPTER 1

The Liturgy of Creation

Joel Payne, Resound Worship

Genesis 1 & 2

A few years ago, my wife and I accidentally took on the rather ambitious task of building our own home. We had secured a dilapidated bungalow on a promising plot and we'd drawn up plans for a refurbishment and major renovation. But, as you've no doubt learnt from repeats of *Grand Designs*, none of these projects ever go smoothly. I vividly remember the day the contractor called us in to show us the shell of the building after he had pulled down the bits we wouldn't need, explaining that it was really not worth keeping. We grimly agreed and, as the digger moved in to knock down the rest, we accepted that we had become accidental house builders with a home that was distinctly 'formless and empty', and it was time to get creative.

I've often puzzled over the opening verses of Genesis, where the earth is described in a similar way. Why does God appear to have begun creation but then paused, or at least the narrative pauses, leaving a formless, empty earth, with 'darkness over the surface of the deep' (v. 2)? What exactly, in the process of creation, is this describing? How does it fit into the chronological or scientific narrative? I think I've been hoping for some kind of geological answer, but I wonder if the author may be addressing a different question altogether.

In the Ancient Near East, many creation myths spoke of an earth born out of conflict between rival gods. While the biblical account was primarily written to assert that the God of Israel is the true creator, it appears it was to tell us more than his identity. It was to tell us his character. The one true God is not a selfish deity whose actions have chaotic consequences. Quite the opposite, he is a good God who creates order from chaos.

Churches have varying relationships with order in worship. Some follow a traditional format that has been handed down through centuries. Others prize spontaneity and new expressions. Yet even the most modern churches usually follow a repeated pattern. The worship service has a beginning, an end, a time for praise, a time for prayer, and time to hear the Scriptures. Another word for this order or journey of worship is liturgy. Ancient or modern, all churches have one.

Old Testament scholar Walter Brueggemann has suggested that the narrative in Genesis 1 may in fact be an ancient liturgy:

> The primary and proper context in which Israel articulated its creation faith is in doxology, the public, liturgical practice of lyrical, poetic utterance whereby Israel sings its awe and wonder about the glory and goodness of God's creation.[1]

We know ancient Scriptures were designed to be read aloud. It is not difficult to imagine this passage being read in public worship. It may even help make sense of the style and the structure of chapter one:

- The leader acts as narrator.
- The choir sings the refrain, 'And there was morning, and there was evening…' (vv. 8, 13, 19, 22, 31).
- The congregation unites in spoken responses, 'And God saw that it was good' (vv. 4, 10, 12, 18, 21, 24), with an ever-increasing intensity until the final shout: 'God saw all that he had made, and it was very good!' (v. 31).

Like any liturgy, it has a beginning and a narrative journey. It also has an end. We might imagine that, having introduced humanity as those who bear the divine image and act as God's royal representatives

1 Brueggemann, Walter, *An Introduction to the Old Testament: The Canon and Christian Imagination* (Louisville: Westminster John Knox, 2003), 34.

in the world, the final exhortation would be to go out and 'live and work to [his] praise and glory'.[2] Especially where words translated as 'rule' and 'subdue' have been used. But this liturgy doesn't end with effort. It ends with rest (2:2-3).

Rest is not easily achieved when you feel there is constant work to be done, when you are sure a thing cannot survive without your perpetual involvement and supervision. When my wife and I completed our house-build, the last project was to transform the remaining building site into a garden. We planted and sowed and toiled, investing in something that would take several years to reach maturity. And while the temptation is to endlessly weed, prune and water, we had to let it do its own thing. The only way to see, and truly enjoy, the results of our labours is to rest.

The explosive liturgy of creation leads us to a place of rest. It is an invitation by God to enjoy all he has made. It is a reminder to trust that the God of order has set something in motion that doesn't require our constant tinkering and supervision. It is already 'very good'.

QUESTIONS FOR REFLECTION & DISCUSSION

1. What do you make of those opening verses of Genesis 1?
2. Do you think of the earth, and all creation, as something intrinsically good? Do you think that goodness remains in all aspects?
3. Do you have any personal experience of God bringing order out of chaos?
4. How would you describe the liturgy of your church? Where is the structure and where is the freedom? How do you relate to those different aspects?
5. When could you take some time to rest and simply enjoy what God has already called 'very good'?

2 As in the traditional post-communion prayer e.g. *Common Worship* (London: Church House Publishing, 2000), 182.

God of immeasurable might,
whose hands shaped the sun in the sky;
on solid foundations established creation
and gave it life.
Everything made by design,
crafted with wisdom divine;
painted with purpose on your living canvas,
making the world come alive!

Praise the Lord, my soul!
God, you are wonderful!
All of creation breathes because of you.
You have poured your heart
into this work of art
and, with breath you gave,
the world responds in praise:
thank you for all you have made!

You are the giver of life,
sustainer of all in your sight;
you care for the needs
of the creatures beneath
your watchful eye.
You're our creator and King,
your goodness surrounds everything;
ruling with kindness and walking beside us,
reigning in majesty.

God Of Immeasurable Might

CHAPTER 2

God's Creativity in Worship

W. David O. Taylor, Fuller Seminary

Psalm 104

In Psalm 104, we encounter a God who creates, not out of any necessity that lies outside of his character, but in freedom and joy. Verse 24 sums up the entire thrust of the psalm: 'What a wildly wonderful world, God! You made it all, with Wisdom at your side, made earth overflow with your wonderful creations.' (*The Message*).

As the church's historic prayer book sees it, creation bears witness to its God-ordained purposes, but its witness is never minimalist or merely pragmatic; instead 'one day is brimming over with talk for the next day' (Ps 19:2). God in turn charges us to be creative as his royal agents, crowned with divine privileges, to make something of the world that God so loves.

What then does God's creativity have to do with creativity in worship? While the answer to this question has generated a good deal of debate throughout church history, I wish to propose three possible answers in what I might call a trinitarian register.

God the Father: Maker of Heaven and Earth

First, the world that God has made is marked by a gracious hyper-abundance. In God's creation, there is an excess of possibilities. Through the wonder of an eighty-eight key piano, for instance, there is the possibility of 309,485,009,821,345,068,724,781,056 chord voicings. In God's world there is *get to*, not just *have to*. We have to build shelters; but we *get to* build basilicas and Gothic cathedrals. We have to give God glory, but we *get to* do so with rock-n-roll anthems and Medieval morality plays.

We get to imagine, like God, new things into being: cassocks, Shaker dances, improvised spirituals, and *The Saint John's Bible*. Because of the abundance that marks God's creation, humans in worship are thus freed from an anxious need to feel only 'useful' or 'practical'.

God the Son: The True Human

Second, while it is only in Christ that we perceive the true image of humanity, it is also only in Christ that we see the extent of humanity's brokenness. In Christ's initiative, to become 'flesh from our flesh', then, we discover the proper shape of our vocation. In Christ we see what is humanly—and thus creatively—possible. As Jesus, for example, uses stories to reveal the human condition, so artists use stories to reveal humanity's glory (Gen 1) and its misery (Gen 3). Or as Jesus enables us to 'sense' the goodness of God, so artists make the goodness of God sensible through sight (Tiffany stained glass windows), sound (Rend Collective's *Joy of the Lord*), taste (freshly made communion bread), touch (a Jewish circle dance), and smell (frankincense issuing from a thurible).

God the Spirit: Lord and Giver of Life

Lastly, in the same way that the Holy Spirit illumines the things of God, so artists bring to light things that are hidden or dim, as with the cry for justice that marks Mary's Magnificat or Urban Doxology's song *God Not Guns*. Just like the Spirit, who exposes the depths of the human condition, so too artists expose the depths of human grief, as the Congolese setting of the Latin Mass, Missa Luba's *Kyrie*, does, while also drawing our attention to the expansiveness of the human imagination, as we witness in Gaudí's *Sagrada Família* architecture. And as the Spirit unites the like and the unlike, so artists bring into relation things that might not have been expected or believed possible, such as the liturgical music of Aradhna which makes use of Classical Indian musical forms.

In the spirit of the psalms and in light of our calling as creatures made in the image of a creative God, liturgical artists are free, I suggest, to make art that, among other things, offers a foretaste of a world put to rights, no longer infected by sin or marked by an economy of scarcity, but marked by an economy of abundance and suffused with grace. And since no style or genre or media can exhaustively express all possible expressions of praise and prayer that befit the Triune God, it will require the whole body of Christ, over the whole course of eternity, to make tangible the glory of our Creator through the art that it produces.

QUESTIONS FOR REFLECTION & DISCUSSION

1. In what way do Psalms 8, 19, 104, and 148 echo and expand upon the language of Genesis 1 and 2?
2. How might the language of Genesis, 'to till and to tend the earth,' which the Psalter links to our worship of God, challenge how you have understood the idea of being stewards of God's creativity in worship?
3. How is your worship charging the imagination of your congregation in such a way that it enables them to perceive the world as God sees it?
4. What are some of the unique flora, fauna, animal life and geological properties of your area, and how might your worship give voice to the praise of God in the creation that surrounds you?
5. What is one new, creative, artistic thing that you might try out in worship with your community?

Let all creation sing before the Lord
and every nation of the earth rejoice,
let all the trees lift a shout of joy
for the Lord is King.
Let the deep waters of the sea resound,
let every mountain, every hill sing out,
let all the fields make a joyful sound
for the Lord is King.

Mighty river, barren desert,
howling wind and stormy weather,
every canyon, every valley,
sing your praise and give him glory.
Nature proclaims the glory of our God,
nature proclaims his name.

Every star and constellation,
every wonder in the heavens,
silver moon and supernova,
sing a shining hallelujah!
Nature proclaims the glory of our God,
nature proclaims his name.

Honey bees and weeping willows,
grizzly bears and armadillos,
every narwhal and sea otter,
every son and every daughter.
Nature proclaims the glory of our God,
nature proclaims his name.

La la la la la la la – All the earth, praise the Lord!
La la la la la la la – All the earth, praise the Lord!

Let All Creation Sing

CHAPTER 3

Worshipping with All Creation

Jeremy Begbie, Duke University

Psalm 148

I write this as the UK is just starting to emerge from the Covid-19 lockdown. Many have told me how in the last few months they have begun to see and hear things they never noticed before. The bird chorale at 5 in the morning, the rippled bark on that beech tree at the bottom of the road, Kermit-green nettles swaying in the wind, bees hovering over wild flowers. As the roar of the roads retreats, and life's pace slows (at least for some of us), we have re-discovered the world around us.

A wise writer said, 'Our lives are made from the things we pay attention to.'[1] Psalm 148 pictures things we've seen a hundred times before (apart from angels, perhaps). Sun, moon, stars, fire, snow, frost—all very familiar. But the psalmist makes us look—not merely see, but look, attend, pay attention to what they're doing.

They all praise God. All creatures—notice how the word 'all' keeps appearing—the totality of things in the heavens (vv. 1-4) and on earth (vv. 7-12). They all praise the Creator.

How? Simply by doing their own thing in their own way. Take 'fruit trees' (v. 9). A fruit tree praises God by being itself, doing what fruit trees do best—growing, flowering, producing fruit. And the same applies to mountains and hills, creeping things and birds—the whole teeming lot. Every day we are surrounded by a vast, uncontainable, ceaseless hymn of praise, each creature glorifying God in its own way. And this is going on whether we see it, hear it, notice it, acknowledge it or not.

1 Jones, Lucy, 'Noticing Nature Is The Greatest Gift You Can Get From Lockdown' in *The Guardian,* 16 May 2020.

Why does the psalmist want us to notice this cosmic praise? Above all, because we're reminded *who is at the centre of things.* It's perilously easy to think creation needs us to praise God, like the vicar who can't believe his people can worship God without him. Here humans are not centre stage. They're only mentioned in the last three verses (11-14). Yes, you and I have a unique role in God's world—we can know we are loved by God, and can magnify and extend the praise of creation—through farming, industry, art and music. But we are not the pivot around which all else revolves. God is the one to be worshipped, and the cat in your sitting room and the robin at the bottom of the garden are quite able to praise God without us.

Just because God is at the centre, then, creation gives us a *model* of praise. Notice the psalmist *invites* creation to praise God: 'let them praise…!' That might seem a little odd, but it's a fitting image: the psalmist is assembling the cosmic orchestra and telling it to play so we can *learn* from it. What does it mean to be a human being praising God? It means doing what we were created to do, not trying to be God. Like the fruit tree, even the wild animals and the cattle (v. 10), we will never be more fully ourselves than when everything resonates with the Composer and speaks of him. Praise is more than a song, it is a way of life.

What this Psalm doesn't give us is any hint of what's gone wrong. There's no mention of nature's cruelty, no destructive disease, no deadly virus. But this is where the New Testament takes us behind the scenes. There we learn that energising and directing this unstoppable praise is Jesus Christ, the one by whom, through whom, and for whom all things were made. We learn that the cosmic praise has turned sour, dissonant with evil. And we learn that the conductor of our praise has come to this world to take on that dissonance, to re-tune us back to God. Through him, a new music is now possible, richer than ever before, a symphony we can start to play now, but will only know beyond death.

'Our lives are made from the things we pay attention to.' Yes, pay attention with the psalmist to creation's praise, but do that by paying attention to the one at the heart of it all. Then our lives will indeed be made—in fact, re-made.

QUESTIONS FOR REFLECTION & DISCUSSION

1. When did you last acknowledge the praise of creation?
2. Why do we often ignore creation's praise?
3. How does, for example, a mountain praise God?
4. What does it mean to lead lives of praise?
5. In light of all this, what is the writer to the Hebrews telling us when he puts the words of Psalm 22 on Jesus' lips: 'In the midst of the congregation I will praise you.' (Heb 2:12)?

Nature shines with beauty,
bringing us a revelation
of the Maker's glory,
leading us in adoration.

O God who made the stars
and formed us from the dust,
your plans are over ours
and all your ways are love.

Nature groans in labour,
longing for the revelation
of the Maker's children
on the day of liberation.

Nature Shines With Beauty

CHAPTER 4

Visions of Worship and Redemption

Chris Juby, Resound Worship

Romans 8

Which chapters of Scripture do you think are most frequently quoted as part of worship? I don't have any hard data, but my church has open contributions during our meetings, and, if we're anything to go by, I think Romans 8 must be a contender. Verse after verse in that chapter powerfully and memorably captures truths about our life in Christ. You can probably fill in the blank for most of these if I start (to name but a few):

'There is now no condemnation…' (v. 1)
'The Spirit you received does not make you slaves…' (v. 15)
'In all things God works for the good…' (v. 28)
'If God is for us…' (v. 31)
'We are more than conquerors…' (v. 37)

These ideas are quoted so often in prayers, readings and song lyrics that you could almost be forgiven for thinking you know exactly what Romans 8 is about. But woven all the way through this chapter is a mysterious and much more neglected thread relating our new life to the rest of creation. Perhaps those of you who quoted the verses above with me, have also joined me in puzzling about this:

> For the creation waits in eager expectation for the children of God to be revealed. For the creation was subjected to frustration, not by its own choice, but by the will of the one who subjected it, in hope that the creation itself will be liberated from its bondage to decay and brought into the freedom and glory of the children of God. (vv. 19-21)

As we wrote songs on the *Doxecology* themes of 'creation, ecology and Christian hope', this passage from Romans 8 kept coming to my mind as having something important to say on the subject. But while clearly profound, it feels much harder to understand than the surrounding verses.

A habit I've got into through leading worship and writing songs for the church is that when I don't understand a passage of Scripture, I bring it before God in worship—putting phrases from the text to music, or simply reading it with an orientation of praise. That approach often leads to a different kind of understanding than when I only try to analyse using the tools of study. Immersed in the rich themes of *Doxecology* that speak of the ways that the rest of creation calls us to worship, I realised that there was a profound correlation between the way in which nature calls us to worship, and the mysterious truth in Romans 8 that our new life calls the rest of creation to hope.

Much is marred in creation because of the Fall, but it still carries such an abundant reflection of the glory of its maker that we are rightly led to worship. And although much remains marred in humanity, those of us in Christ still carry such an abundant reflection of the glory of the maker's plans that the rest of creation is led in hope that everything will one day be renewed.

In God's redeeming mercy, we who caused frustration for our fellow creatures have become a sign of blessing to them instead of a curse. Our old, fallen humanity speaks of what was lost; our new humanity speaks of what is to be gained. This is too high to fully comprehend, and yet utterly characteristic of the God whose love will be overcome by 'neither death nor life, neither angels nor demons, neither the present nor the future, nor any powers, neither height nor depth, nor anything else in all creation.' (vv. 38-39)

QUESTIONS FOR REFLECTION & DISCUSSION

1. Read through Romans 8 again, marking all the mentions of creation. Had you noticed that thread before?
2. Can you put into your own words how the longing of creation in verse 19 relates to the rest of the chapter?
3. How do you feel about the idea of being led in worship by the rest of creation?
4. What do you think it means for us to be a sign of hope for the rest of creation? How does it affect the way we live if we think in those terms?
5. Is there a passage of Scripture that you're wrestling with? How could you give voice to that before God in worship?

Part Two
The Cry of Creation

Hear the song of our lament,
we grieve a dry and broken land;
hearts have turned from your intent
and earth is ravaged by our hand.

Oceans weep for beauty lost,
and forests plead for your return,
fields are drenched in tears and blood;
all nature groans beneath sin's curse.

Have mercy,
have mercy,
have mercy on us, Lord.
Renew us,
restore us,
have mercy on us, Lord.

Peoples rage and nations rise
to war and waste for senseless gain,
turning from creation's cries
and trading glory in for shame.

Lead us in your Eden call
to live as those who bear your name;
show us how to love your world
until the day you come again.

Hear The Song Of Our Lament

CHAPTER 5

Crying with Creation

Rachel Wilhelm, United Adoration

Psalm 102

Lament is an honest prayer and cry for help in suffering, in the face of an injustice, failure, or crisis. The posture of lament is faith, even though the one lamenting feels doubtful, or angry, or sorrowful, because lament is aimed toward the only one who has the power to fix the problem.

Since the Fall, the disease of sin has had its way in all of creation. In Romans 8:22 it says 'all creation has been groaning […] right up to the present time.' There is an understanding that there is something not right or missing from creation; a certainty that the cycle of life to death will come as it always does, and we, as part of God's creation, take part. We cannot help but reflect what all of creation is already doing by yearning for the hope of glory, and for the time when we get to sing a song of redemption and praise in the presence of God in a new heavens and new earth.

I worry a lot. Since having children, the tendency has gotten a little worse, given that there are some things that are simply out of my immediate control (but really, what control do I really have?). Through learning the hard way, I found that making God my first phone call, instead of fretting before friends or family, was the most effective way to order my struggles. I was able to see the rhythm of lament many times after I stepped into the car and started with, 'God, please hear me. I need you. I beg you to see me.' Naturally I would launch into the details of my suffering, hashing it out, asking God questions, expressing my fear or doubt in the open. After exhausting myself with the enormity of my sorrow, the situation felt hopeless, and I would be out of words to state my case. The only option, as God and I were together, was for me to remind God of who he is, the promises he's made, and ask him to move in my situation. By reminding God of who he is, the natural flow would turn quickly to praise of him and my faith would be strengthened, believing that the God I take my complaint to hears me; and is able to act.

In Psalm 102, there seem to be four sections:

1. The demand or cry (vv. 1-2).
2. The suffering complaint (vv. 3-11).
3. The recalling of God's work and promises and calling him to action (vv. 12-22).
4. The praise of God and what is true about him (vv. 23-28).

The beautiful thing the psalmist does in this particular psalm, and there are so many others like it, is he likens his suffering to the decay of creation, or uses creation to emphasise his affliction. For example, 'my bones burn like glowing embers' (v. 3) or 'my heart is blighted and withered like grass,' (v. 4). There is an understanding in the Psalms that humanity is connected to all of creation, moving together in a constant cycle of birth, life, withering, and death. All creation is praising God constantly, and yet, in the midst of the praise, creation knows that it is yearning for a coming time when it will be made new.

We don't think about this. We don't see ourselves as part of this cycle of lament that creation constantly runs through; but through the Psalms, God uses creation to teach us how to praise, and how to lament, and how to be aware of our humanity and depravity. Creation needs God, just as we do. All of nature shows itself dependent on him as long as the sun and moon endure, yet we so easily believe God does not want to be involved in *that* part of our lives. We sanitise our prayers while a lion eats a zebra and a flood drowns the land, or a fire burns up a forest. God works in all of the goings on of nature, and through the decay, in his faithfulness, comes life.

I urge you to come to God in your mess. Demand he hear you. Tell him your complaint. After you can't say any more about your situation, remember God's faithful deeds and remember that only he can act.

Then praise him, knowing this, because he brings all things together for good under his lordship: even creation, even your soul.

QUESTIONS FOR REFLECTION & DISCUSSION

1. Read through Psalm 102. In what ways does the psalmist pair creation with a state of human suffering?
2. How is lament an act of faith?
3. How do we reflect what creation 'is already doing' in the world?
4. How do the Psalms teach us to order our emotions in a healthy way?
5. How does creation lament? What can we learn from creation about being emotionally honest with God about our suffering?

If the fields are parched
and the trees are felled
will the rocks cry aloud on their own?
If the birds are starved
and the beasts are killed
will the bones in the dust lift a song?

Have mercy, Lord,
have mercy, Lord.
Forgive our broken ways.
Have mercy, Lord,
have mercy, Lord.
Renew the world you made.

As the oceans rise
and the wells run dry
do we care if disaster is near?
If our children starve
will they cry to God?
Will they curse us for closing our ears?

Still a day will come
when the Lord returns
and the earth will be perfect again.
No more greed or war,
no more tooth and claw,
for the wolf and the lamb will be friends.

If The Fields Are Parched (Have Mercy)

CHAPTER 6

Confession for the Climate

Jeremy Williams, Christian Climate Action

Ezekiel 37:1–14

On Easter Sunday of 2019, I got up and made the kids their breakfast. I had every intention of going to the morning service at church but another event was calling for my attention. That week, Extinction Rebellion were occupying a number of sites in London, demanding action on climate change. Later that week Parliament would declare a climate emergency, and by the end of the year Britain would announce a new target to be carbon neutral by 2050. But at that point, it was all on the line.

Christian Climate Action—the Christians in Extinction Rebellion—were right on the front lines of this movement. They too were hosting an Easter Sunday morning service, in the middle of the road at Marble Arch, and it would be crowd-sourced: anybody could bring a contribution. I knew where I wanted to be.

I asked God if there was anything I should say. Ezekiel 37 came to mind, and we jumped on the train.

Ezekiel, like Jeremiah, is a prophet who warns about the impending incursion of the Babylonians, and that Israel will be carried away into exile. Ezekiel takes his message to the streets with acts of guerrilla theatre that would probably fit in well in Extinction Rebellion circles. And his message is not a happy one. He is literally a prophet of doom. 'The end! The end has come,' God tells Ezekiel to prophesy. 'Doom has come upon you, upon you who dwell in the land.' (Ezek 7:2, 7).

Though the immediate threat is the Babylonians, the doom that Ezekiel foretells is often ecological. He describes famine and flood and forest fires, all consequences of runaway climate change that we see in evidence today (Ezek 20:47). There are even 'cities no longer inhabited' because the oceans have risen up and closed over them, a strange echo of sea-level rise (Ezek 26:19). As an environmental campaigner, I cannot read Ezekiel without seeing climate change all through it.

This is no direct parallel, of course. Ezekiel is not about climate change. And I don't believe that the breakdown of the climate is a punishment from God. But what we see in climate change is nevertheless a breakdown in covenant. The relationship between people and the earth has been broken. Humanity has failed to heed the basic purpose for which we were made, to work and care for the earth (Gen 2:15). Or more specifically, those of us in the industrialised nations of the global North have failed. In doing so we have taken more than our fair share of the earth's resources, and dumped more than our fair share of pollution into the atmosphere. We have failed to love our global neighbours, and ignored the suffering of the world's most vulnerable.

What to do then, when 'the fields are parched, and the trees are felled'? We have to come to God again. 'Have mercy, Lord. Forgive our broken ways.'

Ecological destruction should call us to confession, to admit that we have overshot the good and natural limits of the biosphere. We have been greedy and put our own needs above those of others, including future generations. A call for forgiveness is empty words unless it also includes repentance, and a commitment to live differently. It should call us to work for the renewal of the earth, and to restore what has been unjustly taken from others.

For Ezekiel, it was too late. The Babylonians came, and parts of the book are written from exile. There was no stopping it, and Israel was destroyed. For us, it is also too late. It is too late to prevent climate change– there are people living through the fire and the floods right now. But it is not too late to avert complete destruction. There is still hope that the worst effects of climate change can be avoided, if we act in time.

Despite the message of doom, there is hope in Ezekiel too. Standing before the bleached bones of a fallen army, God tells Ezekiel to prophesy, and the bones reconnect. Muscles and skin regrow, and Ezekiel sees an incredible vision of regeneration, even when 'our bones are dried up and our hope is gone' (Ezek 37:11).

That Easter Sunday, I preached in the street at Marble Arch from Ezekiel 37. 'Death does not get the final word!' I shouted, surrounded by the brightly coloured sand-timer flags of Extinction Rebellion. 'Extinction cannot have the final word! The spirit of Jesus infuses the universe, and it is a spirit of resurrection.'

QUESTIONS FOR REFLECTION & DISCUSSION

1. Why does God ask Ezekiel if the bones can live? And what do you make of Ezekiel's answer?
2. God could speak over the bones, but he gets Ezekiel to do it. Why might that be?
3. What ecological sins do we need to confess?
4. What broken ways do we need to turn from as we repent?
5. How can we bring resurrection to the environment?

Where are you, in the storm,
in the chaos can you hear
our desperate call?
Water rising, are you sleeping:
are you Lord after all?

Where are you, in the rain?
Earth is crying
for an end to all its pain.
We are sinking, heaven weeping:
will we see light again?

In the storm, you're the anchor,
you are our hope, you are the shield.
Every rainbow a promise:
you love this world,
all of creation will be healed.

O speak your mighty word;
raging waters will bow down
before their Lord.
Peace commanding, promise keeping,
of a planet restored.

Where Are You In The Storm

CHAPTER 7

Signs of God in the Chaos

Sam Hargreaves, engageworship

Luke 8:22-25

Living in England, I find it easy to romanticise the natural world. Our hills are green and pleasant, our rivers and lakes generally small and gentle, and our animals are usually pretty tame. It is not surprising, then, that so much of our 'natural theology' (and our worship songs) reflects on how creation displays God's beauty, order and peace.

For most of the world this is far from their experience. A friend told me that, growing up in India, nature was seen as a powerful, dangerous thing that humanity had to battle with and subdue. In many countries the wild animals can kill you; the mountains, deserts and jungles are similarly places of threat and fear.

In Bible times we see a similar concern about the natural world and this is well demonstrated by stories about seas and storms. Many characters are caught up in life-threatening storms—Jonah, Noah and Paul spring to mind.

The climate crisis is a time for British (and other Western) Christians to begin to comprehend the power and danger of the natural world. The once-tame elements have responded to our careless intervention. Physical storms have battered our towns. Sea levels and global temperatures are rising. In the face of this we feel helpless. We might begin to wonder: where is God? Is he asleep like Jesus on Lake Galilee, snoozing while we drift towards catastrophe?

It is worth remembering that storms have multiple functions in Bible stories. They do show the dangers of the earth and the frailty of humankind, and they call disobedient followers to repent. But they are also places where God reveals his glory and power to his people. The psalmist writes: 'You rule over the surging sea; when its waves mount up, you still them', and 'Mightier than the thunder of the great waters, mightier than the breakers of the sea— the Lord on high is mighty.' (Ps 89:9, 93:4, see also 107:23-30).

For Jesus to stand and calm the storm with a word—this is more than just a merciful miracle. It is a revelation of his true nature. When the disciples ask, 'Who is this?' they imply an unspoken answer: this Jesus is God. This man, sleeping in their boat, walking with them daily, is at the same time the Lord of heaven and earth, the only one with power and authority to subdue nature.

Our God reveals himself in many ways—his word, his world, and through many symbols and signs. The sign of revelation after Noah's flood was a rainbow—a promise drawn across the sky for all the creatures of the earth. God declared that he was making this covenant 'with every living creature that was with you—the birds, the livestock and all the wild animals' (Gen 9:10). It was a promise and sign that never again would he flood the earth: never again would he cleanse creation with a storm.

The covenant made through Jesus was symbolised not with a rainbow, but with bread and wine. These are very ordinary, everyday objects for many people, fruit of the ground and harvest of the fields, things that we share daily. Yet Jesus takes these familiar things and makes them a revelation of who he is and what he is doing in the world. They are a part of our worship that gives us a tactile, edible reminder of how God works through the physical things of earth. He affirms what he has made and uses it as a way of revealing his heart for restoring all things.

As we engage worshipfully with God's creation we will be reminded that, beyond beauty and peace, God has other messages for us. When we feel afraid because of change and chaos around us, we can call out to the creator as the disciples did in the boat. We can trust in his covenant promises to protect, renew and restore the earth. We can have our eyes opened by signs and symbols to a deeper revelation of God's power, love and redemptive plan.

QUESTIONS FOR REFLECTION & DISCUSSION

1. In what ways are you prone to romanticising the natural world?
2. What feels to you like 'chaos' and 'storm' in the wider creation?
3. What would it look like for you to call out to God for him to be at work in the creation we have mistreated?
4. Look again at God's covenant with Noah. Does this give you fresh insight into God's care for animals?
5. Have you thought about the connection between bread and wine and Jesus' restoration of all creation?

Why are you downcast, O my soul,
so full of fear where once was hope?
Remember God still loves the world:
be still, my soul.

Beneath the shadow of each storm,
in all the sorrow and despair,
Remember God still loves the world:
be still, my soul.

Be still, my soul,
trust in your God,
his perfect ways,
his endless love.
Be still and know
he reigns above the earth.
Be still, my soul,
be still, me soul.

In all your striving, find his peace,
become a shining light of grace
and show that God still loves the world:
be still, my soul.

Be Still My Soul

CHAPTER 8

Dealing with Despair

Sara Hargreaves, engageworship

Psalm 42

I remember an occasion a couple of years ago during a book group meeting. We were discussing which genres of literature we prefer, and I was singing the praises of dystopian sci-fi—my favourite. My friend looked at me over her glass of wine and commented, 'Well, you clearly don't read enough books about climate change!' I remember an icy lump forming in the pit of my stomach. My friend's voice was full of anxiety—she had read many books on climate change, and dystopian sci-fi was often too close to the truth, she told me. I remember carrying that icy lump with me for weeks afterwards.

You may well feel that same cold fear in your inner being when climate change comes up in conversation. It's a right response. Fear is our bodies' warning system. 'You're walking too close to the edge of the cliff —step back!' it tells us, or 'That dog looks aggressive, run away!' We need fear to warn us of the dangers involved in climate change.

Fear—as any emotion—is also designed to be contagious. If a big bear is running into our village, it's helpful if the person spotting the bear first is able to quickly make everyone else in the village scared, and so take action. When you read a news report about climate change by a petrified journalist—yes, you are going to feel scared.

As Christians, however, this response often triggers a sense of guilt. Surely we're not supposed to feel scared? Isn't 'Do not be afraid' one of God's most repeated commands in the Bible? So we often bury our fear, pretending it isn't there and walking around with a constant low-level anxiety playing in the background instead. We might notice that we are not as happy as we once were. 'Why, my soul, are you downcast? Why so disturbed within me?' (v. 5) Lack of joy also feels wrong to admit as Christians, so we often try to distract ourselves by singing our triumphant songs a little louder.

When we experience fear, sadness or anger, we might find that our previous ways of praying and worshipping God stop working so well. We might think back, much like the psalmist in verse 4, to times when we were able to worship God with shouts of joy and praise together with our congregations. We remember those days fondly. Perhaps we were younger and life was less complicated, we think; perhaps that kind of worship is not possible for adults who know too much?

The writers of the psalms did not have consultant psychologists to check their work over, yet they seem to get many things right in their approach to prayer and worship. Here are some ways we can learn from them:

Acknowledge the Emotion

The psalmists are angry to the point of raging, fearful to the point of paralysis and sad to the point of depression. Some of the things they write seem inappropriate to us, but they express them nonetheless. Psychologists today tell us we need to notice our emotions, acknowledge them and sit with them. There is no other way to move forward. If we don't, the results include symptoms like the inability to feel joy, symptoms of stress, physical ill health and depression, to name a few.

Allow Joy to Take Turns

Children naturally allow joy into the midst of a sad or scary time, they can cry one moment and laugh the next. As adults we often think that if something is bad, we are only allowed to feel bad. The psalmists have this remarkable turn-taking ability, to have great sadness (v. 3) mingled with great joy and trust (v. 8). We can learn to look for the goodness in the midst of bad. We can trust that 'God still loves the world', and feel joy over his unchanging love.

Still Yourself

Psalm 46 verse 10 feels like my life verse: 'Be still and know that I am God.' If I don't stop; if I keep distracting myself with social media, busy-ness and inhibitory emotions like anxiety, I remain as 'god' of my life. But if I still myself, if I reject the distractions and sit in silence and in contemplative prayer, I am made aware that God is God, I am not. And that knowledge has vast-reaching consequences. He is able to carry my heavy burdens of sadness and fear, he is strong enough to hear my angry rants, he is loving enough to carry me through.

A crisis in our world can make us all feel helpless and afraid, and that fear is right and important. But it is the beginning of our response before the God who still loves the world, not the end.

QUESTIONS FOR REFLECTION & DISCUSSION

1. Do you think that some emotions are appropriate or inappropriate within Christian worship?
2. Do you know of any songs or prayers that successfully express the sentiments of Psalm 42?
3. How can you personally, and also as part of corporate worship, acknowledge the difficult emotions like fear, sadness and anger?
4. When you consider the challenge of the climate crisis, how can you allow joy to take turns with the bad? Are there characteristics of God you particularly need to remind yourself of?
5. Do you find it difficult to be still before God? How could you grow in your experience of contemplative prayer?

Part Three

The Hope of Creation

At your bidding there was beginning,
at your summons this world was formed,
all things living brought into being
by the power of your word.
You saw that it was good,
you saw that it was good,
help us give you thanks
with the praise and awe we should.

For all your ways are good,
yes, all your ways are good;
God of all creation,
all your ways are good.

In this garden that you have given,
we were hungry for all its fruit,
so we plundered the earth and oceans,
seizing more than we were due.
We stole from what was good,
we stole from what was good,
help us face the truth
with the honesty we should.

As the planet longs for redemption,
spoiled and reeling from nature's loss,
we remember the source of healing
flowing out from Jesus' cross.
You came down for our good,
you came down for our good,
help us look to you
with the hope and faith we should.

If we bow down and seek your mercy,
will you hear us and still forgive?
Holy Spirit, make us determined
to reshape the way we live.
Restore all that is good,
restore all that is good,
help us change our hearts
so we show the care we should.

You Saw That It Was Good

CHAPTER 9

The Cross and Creation

Dave Bookless, A Rocha International

Colossians 1:15-23

How it is that a weapon of torture, terror and murder becomes a symbol of hope and an aid to worship? There have occasionally been hymns and songs almost glamourising the cross, turning it into a cosy source of comfort and consolation. Surely, however, our starting point must be the bleakness and despair of a broken body on a broken tree? Splintered wood, bloody wounds, broken flesh, ominous skies, despair and desolation. All that God made so very good ripped to shreds. The carpenter nailed to a crude wooden scaffold. The Son of God, the co-creator, lynched and killed by his own creatures. Only as we enter the utter God-forsakenness and tragedy of the cross can we really understand its mysterious power and majestic scope. Only this crucified God can truly enter into the wounds and agonies of broken and scarred people in a distorted and polluted world.

In Colossians 1 we find a stunning prayer-poem of worship that takes us on a journey with the cross of Christ, from personal rescue and redemption (vv. 13-14), to cosmic reconciliation (vv. 15-20), and back to personal response and rejoicing (vv. 21-29). This is a journey that is common to much authentic worship. Our first response to God's mercy in Christ is deeply personal. He died and suffered *for me?*

We are awestruck and overwhelmed that Jesus loves us so much, that the agony he underwent was for us. We are deeply aware of our sin that nailed him to the cross, and of the love that held him there. But as we contemplate the cross, God invites us deeper into its mystery. Jesus died not only for me, not only for all other people, but 'to reconcile to himself all things, whether things on earth or things in heaven, by making peace through his blood, shed on the cross' (v. 20). In other words, the cross is much larger than personal salvation. It is also about cosmic reconciliation. In verses 15-20 we see that Jesus is himself the creator: powers and possibilities, gerbils and goldfish, mountains and molehills were all created not just through him but *for* him (v. 16). Biodiversity, the extravagant variety of life with which we share this fragile planet, was made *for* Jesus.

Moreover, we learn Jesus is not just the source of creation but its sustainer: 'in him all things hold together' (v. 17). He gives coherence and purpose to God's ongoing project of creation, and sustains it by his power. The inverse of the truth that all things hold together in him is that all things fall apart without him. Worshipping anything other than Jesus is idolatry. Today's multiple ecological crises have their roots in a failure to worship aright: 'Jesus is Lord!' is a statement with profound environmental implications.

Now, in verse 20, the full scope of the cross becomes clear. It stands at the centre, the crossroads, of God's plan to put right all that began to unravel in Eden. The trees God created very good included the tree we chose to misuse and eat from in a recurring act of self-worship. Yet God never gives up on his people or his creation. Prophets proclaimed new growth from a lifeless tree stump. Now the broken tree of Calvary becomes the source of God's restoring love for all creation. Creation cannot help reacting, in eclipse and earthquake, as its creator, sustainer and Saviour is murdered. Creation today still groans in agonised anticipation of its final liberation from bondage to decay (Rom 8:19-22).

Today, we look to the future, when 'the time comes for God to restore everything' (Acts 3:21), as Jesus returns as Lord of earth and heaven. In our worship now we adore the one who takes all that is alienated, polluted and corrupted, and in his broken body on the cross reconciles and restores it all. In the splintered wood we see the hope of new trees planted to bring healing to the nations and the abundant fruit of God's renewal of creation. We fall on our knees as we glimpse the scope and wonder of the cross.

Thank you, Lord Jesus, for your holy cross, by which you have reconciled the world to yourself. May we worship you with hearts and lives in how we cherish your world.

QUESTIONS FOR REFLECTION & DISCUSSION

1. How big is your understanding of the scope of what Jesus did on the cross?
2. How can we hold together the personal (he died for me) and the cosmic (he died for all creation)?
3. What signs of the agony and brokenness of the cross do you see in creation today?
4. If the cross brings hope from despair, how does that affect our attitudes to (and prayers concerning) today's environmental crises?
5. What does it look like to allow Jesus to be Lord, and worship him for all he did on the cross, in how we eat, recycle, travel and treat God's creation?

As the seeds are planted,
let them yield a harvest,
when the crops are gathered:
let the earth find rest.

As the workers labour,
they deserve their wages,
let them feast with gladness:
let the earth find rest.

Let the earth find rest
as the Lord provides,
till the day of perfect peace;
for the Lord is good
and his love endures
and his mercies never cease.

When the wealthy prosper,
may their hearts be generous,
let them hate injustice:
let the earth find rest.

Let The Earth Find Rest

CHAPTER 10

Sabbath Rest for the Earth

Chris Juby, Resound Worship

Leviticus 25

No one who reads Scripture can escape the challenge that how we live our lives and how we use our money are as important a part of our worship as our gatherings and our songs. See Amos 5:21-24 if you're in any doubt. Worship has an economic aspect.

The issue is not just about what we give to church or to charity. There's also a sense in which every time we use our resources, we vote for the kind of world we want to live in. Do we buy from this business or that business? Do we want to live in a world where poverty is alleviated and our fellow creatures are allowed to thrive, or do we want to live in a world where sweatshops and deforestation are a necessary means to an end? More importantly, what does God require of us?

These are not new questions. Sweatshops and deforestation are contemporary manifestations, but the same underlying issues have been at play in every culture and every generation. Human beings are always tempted to get ahead by trampling the poor and exploiting the land. And God has made it abundantly clear that right worship involves resisting that temptation and ordering our economic lives very differently.

The principles of Sabbath and Jubilee outlined in Leviticus 25 offer a specific picture of that different way. The principle of Sabbath states that every seventh year, the earth should be rested from farming, and everyone—landowner and workers alike—should share 'whatever the land yields' (v. 6). Every fiftieth year was to be a Year of Jubilee, when in addition to another year of Sabbath, all land that had been sold was to return to the original family. Observing those customs would have a powerful effect in restraining poverty and exploitation.

The message of Leviticus that the land should be allowed to rest chimes with that of environnmental campaigners who call on us to cease our careless pillaging of the earth's resources and to allow nature's own processes of restoration to take action unhindered.

But it is very hard to fight against our own greed. Commentators note that there's no evidence that the Year of Jubilee was ever practised. So, what can we do?

A short study like this can't get very far in answering. We each need to ask the Holy Spirit to bring conviction about how we should live our lives. But allow me to share one insight I gained as I wrote the song *Let The Earth Find Rest* from this passage.

I realised that much of the temptation towards greed I find within myself is rooted in a feeling that I need to strive and scheme to get my fair share. That feeling overrides my deeper convictions about what kind of world I want to live in and opens me up to acting in exploitative ways.

The antidote is not to rebuke myself increasingly harshly for my greed. A better way—I find—is to practise gratitude. I deliberately thank God for the blessings in my life and I affirm my trust in his provision. When I experience my life as being characterised by God's overwhelming generosity, I'm much more minded towards generosity to the world around me. Right worship of all kinds overflows.

For that reason, while each verse of *Let The Earth Find Rest* names specific issues of justice from the Scriptures, the chorus dwells on the goodness of God. God spends his resources with unfailing generosity and—thankfully—in the end, *he* will get the world that *he* wants.

Let the earth find rest
as the Lord provides,
till the day of perfect peace;
for the Lord is good
and his love endures
and his mercies never cease.

QUESTIONS FOR REFLECTION & DISCUSSION

1. Why do you think we have no record of the Year of Jubilee ever being practised? Can you imagine any such practice today?
2. If the way you use your resources is a vote for the kind of world you want to live in, what are you voting for?
3. Can you think of any personal practices of Sabbath or Jubilee that might be healthy for you to adopt?
4. How much do you relate to feeling the need to 'strive and scheme to get my fair share'? Are there other factors that hold you back from living generously and justly?
5. How much is your life characterised by gratitude to God? Is there anything you could do to encourage that?

We are the tenants of the King,
we are the workers in his garden,
so we will live and love and care
for this the planet that we share.

We bear the image of our God
and we are sharing in his mission,
so we will follow as we serve,
to see the healing of the earth.

As we wait for the dawning of the day
when the King is coming,
we will live for his glory
and his praise.

For in the victory of the cross
we have a hope of restoration,
all things together under Christ,
a world of flourishing and life.

So fill us up and lead us on
to see the coming of your kingdom,
and we will labour as we sing
for we're the tenants of the King.

We Are The Tenants Of The King

CHAPTER 11

Tenants in God's Kingdom

Jack Wakefield, Tearfund

Romans 12:1–2

When I first moved into my flat, I assumed it was the landlord's job to fix everything. Washing machine clogged? Email the landlord. Bathroom light bulb blown? Email the landlord. It seems ridiculous now, but I hadn't really considered that this was my home and that my housemates and I had a role in looking after it. Thank goodness for a gracious landlord!

My journey of following Jesus has shared a similar learning curve. When I first heard the gospel, it was all about me. I'd sinned? Jesus sorted it. I want to go to heaven? Jesus sorted it. It was an individualistic gospel, a ticket to the after-life, and I could easily substitute my name into John 3:16 without anything changing. For God so loved Jack.

But when I came to learn about the scale of injustice in the world around me, and the brokenness we see in creation, I wondered what relevance this gospel had. What's the good news for people struggling to feed their families, or for the refugees fleeing storms, sea-level rise and other consequences of the climate crisis? Where is God in all of this brokenness?

It was then that I had a perspective shift. The gospel wasn't just about me and my relationship with God after all. The story was far bigger than I ever imagined. I discovered that, throughout the Bible, we meet a God with a mission. The world has been corrupted and broken by sin, but God is on a mission to make all things new, to bring restoration and *shalom*—a transformational concept of peace, wholeness, justice and goodness. Colossians 1:20 says that through Jesus, God is reconciling 'all things, whether things on earth or things in heaven ,by making peace through his blood shed on the cross'. The mission of God is about restoring my relationship with him, but about so much more too: it's about restored relationships between God, humanity and all of creation. It's a mission to see everything God has made, all things on earth and in heaven, experiencing that peace and restoration.

What's more, this God with a mission extends the most incredible invitation to us: come follow me, come and be active tenants, stewards, and co-workers (1 Cor 3:9) in this mission. This gospel is far bigger and far more exciting than I had ever imagined. Not only is God at work, but he invites me to play a part in his story.

Just as it once dawned on me that I was a tenant with responsibilities, so we need to recognise that we are tenants like those Jesus once described in a parable (Mt 21:33-44). Being tenants of the King involves each of us going through a similar perspective shift, increasingly seeing ourselves as participants in the mission of God and discovering how our whole lives can be offered in worship.

In Romans 12:2 Paul warns us not to conform to the broken patterns of society, but instead to keep our eyes fixed on Jesus, aligning ourselves with his values and mission. To do so, Paul says we should be 'transformed by the renewing of [our] minds'. As we align ourselves to the mission of God more and more, we find ourselves redirected: away from the broken patterns of this world and towards the vision of the kingdom of God. Every decision and action becomes an opportunity to bring glory to God and to participate in his mission. Indeed, we learn how our whole lives can be offered in worship!

In the previous verse in Romans 12, Paul urges us to offer our whole lives as a sacrifice. At the same time as encouraging that internal transformation, he says true and proper worship is lived out in our actions. *The Message* paraphrases this verse as: 'Take your everyday, ordinary life—your sleeping, eating, going-to-work, and walking-around life—and place it before God as an offering.' Could there be a better description of what it means to be active tenants in God's world?

This isn't a new idea, of course. About 800 years earlier, in response to broken and unjust patterns of his society, Amos cried: 'Away with the noise of your songs! [...] but let justice roll on like a river' (Amos 5:23-24). Each of us can choose to be tenants of the King, to be people who offer our whole lives as a sacrifice—all our eating, travelling and working—in worship to the God with a mission, honouring him by living lightly on the earth, by loving our neighbours and by caring for his creation. Let's respond to his invitation!

QUESTIONS FOR REFLECTION & DISCUSSION

1. Can you relate to the experience of hearing a limited and individualistic gospel?
2. How does understanding God's mission change the way you see your own life?
3. If Paul were writing today, what might he describe as some of the broken patterns of the world?
4. Have you ever considered your response to the climate crisis as an act of worship?
5. In what ways could you change your 'eating, travelling and working' to worship God and better care for his creation?

God, the maker of the heavens,
and the planet that we share,
show us how to live, like Jesus,
lives of gratitude and care.
Make us mindful of the footprints
from the lives that we pursue.
Make us partners in your mission:
you are making all things new.

God, the gardener of Eden,
teach us how to tend this earth,
learning from the changing seasons,
times of fallow and new birth.
Lord ,have mercy when we're careless,
rich resources we misuse.
Use our hands to heal creation:
you are making all things new.

God of labour and vocation,
Lord of science, trade and art,
take our efforts and our passions
make them mirrors of your heart.
Every habitat and creature
loved and valued, God, by you.
May our lives reveal your kingdom:
you are making all things new.

You are making all things new,
you are making all things new,
all things renewed!

God The Maker Of The Heavens

CHAPTER 12

All Things Renewed

Sam Hargreaves, engageworship

2 Peter 3:11-13

A couple of years ago we bought an old dining-room table. We unscrewed all the pieces, stripped off the battered varnish, sanded the rough edges and added layers of wax finish. Now reconstructed in our dining room, it is a table we gather around daily to eat, do homework, play games and connect. It is a piece of furniture that will last us for years to come. Of course, we could have saved a lot of time by just going to a shop and buying a new table. But for us this was something better—a *renewed* table, not wasting the earth's resources but recycling and restoring something which had existed before and could have a new life with our family.

Listening to many popular worship songs, you would think that our eternity with God will be a purely spiritual existence, very possibly singing songs in heaven on an endless loop. The implication is that we will leave this planet behind, and it therefore doesn't matter how we live on earth now.[1] In contrast, the writers of the New Testament describe our future hope quite differently:

> You ought to live holy and godly lives as you look forward to the day of God and speed its coming. [...] we are looking forward to a *new heaven and a new earth*, where righteousness dwells. (2 Pet 3:11-13, *italics* added)

> Then I saw 'a *new heaven and a new earth*,' for the first heaven and the first earth had passed away, and there was no longer any sea. (Rev 21:1, *italics* added)

1 We analysed the top 25 CCLI songs in the UK and USA along these lines in Hargreaves, Sara & Sam, *Whole Life Worship* (IVP, 2017), chapter 6.

According to Peter and John, our glorious eternity is *on earth with God*, on an earth made new. And the nature of that 'new' is very important. One Greek word for new is *neo*—something new which did not exist before. But that is not the word used in these two passages. The Greek word here is *kainos*. *Kainos* also means new, but it describes something that has a new character, or is renewed.

Neo is buying a new table. *Kainos* is restoring an old table. *Neo* is fast-fashion purchased each new season, chucking the old trends into landfill. *Kainos* is charity-shop vintage, up-cycling old jeans into shorts, repurposing old fabric for new garments. *Neo* is thinking that this old world is going to be destroyed anyway, so what's the point of caring for creation? *Kainos* is believing that God wants us to partner with him in restoring creation, so that what we do to renew creation now matters.

It may be true that the evil, unjust and sinful aspects of our present world will be 'burnt up' (2 Pet 3:12), or 'pass away' (Rev 21:1). Indeed, the Bible often talks of God's judgement as refining—a fire that cleanses and purifies so the gold is left intact, a flood that washes the earth of sin and leaves the righteous. But you, as a Christian, are a new (*kainos*) creation (2 Cor 5:17). You have not been vapourised into non-existence and newly created; rather ,the old has passed away, and the renewed (*kainos*) has come.

Like Jesus' resurrection body, all creation will be resurrected. It will all be renewed. Every part of life on earth is important to God and has the potential to be used and perfected by him. And that means how we live on earth now *matters*. Peter's exhortation to live 'holy and godly lives' means more than keeping our thoughts pure and avoiding swear words. It includes things like how we spend our money, treat the planet, and act in society. It involves cooperating with God as we use our skills, passions and vocations to bless and improve the world around us. These things are not peripheral to the spiritual life—they are an integral part of our discipleship and our worship.

If these things are central, we need to sing about them! The lyrics of our worship songs subtly teach us things about God and his priorities. If we only ever sing about feeling God's presence in church, or only focus on a spiritual eternity in heaven, those are the things we will believe God values. But if we sing about creation, and the world's resources, and very everyday things like 'science, trade and art', we might start to see that these things too matter to God. We might start to celebrate and value the whole creation, and in so doing join with God in making all things new.

QUESTIONS FOR REFLECTION & DISCUSSION

1. Do you know any worship songs or hymns which talk about the daily realities of living on earth? Why do you think we struggle to sing these regularly in church?
2. When you picture eternity with God, what does it look like? Does your picture match Revelation 21 and 22?
3. What difference might it make to your everyday life to think that God will renew all creation?
4. Can you think of examples in your own life of *neo* and *kainos*? Are there ways we could cooperate with God's *kainos*?
5. 'Take our efforts and our passions'—how can you cooperate with God as you engage in your skills, work and hobbies?

God, the Word of life, created all,
sun and moon and galaxies beyond,
giving life to all that lives and breathes,
grace and love supplying every need.
Yet we wait for the day.

In Christ we hope,
by faith we know
our redemption is close,
but still the earth groans.

God, our hope, has heard creation call,
pouring out his mercy on the earth,
giving us his one and only Son
rescuing the world he loves so much.
Yet we wait for the day.

The earth will be healed,
creation set free,
in the great day of the Lord.
The whole earth restored,
in beauty and awe,
in the great day of the Lord

Great Day

CHAPTER 13

The Perfect Worship of Heaven

Joel Payne, Resound Worship

Revelation 4 & 5

When I worked as a full-time worship pastor I developed some rather perfectionist tendencies when it came to planning services. The songs had to say just the right things, with a certain flow between them, relating to the scripture readings in particular ways, and so on. I would spend hours attempting to plan the perfect worship service, weighing up every possible option before making my selections. It clearly wasn't a very healthy approach. More significantly it was an impossible task in the first place! The worship we offer on earth, whether in church gatherings or our everyday lives, is subject to frustration, incomplete until the final restoration of all things. But this is not to say we cannot *aspire* to a higher standard. The Bible does give us a glimpse of corporate worship around which we might model our efforts.

Let's be honest. The book of Revelation—John's account of his vision on the island of Patmos—is a tricky read. Written in an apocalyptic genre, it is full of symbolism and hyperbole. To further complicate things, it has a fairly convoluted chronology. Though none of this seems to stop certain authors and preachers pronouncing they have cracked the code with certainty, we ought to at least approach it with some caution.

Most agree, however, that the scene in chapter four is unambiguously one of perfect heavenly worship. Where worship on earth is marred, worship in the heavenly court is perfect and a model after which we might fashion our own efforts. The scene centres on a throne, on which God himself is seated. Around the throne are twenty-four elders and, within that circle – closest to the throne – are four living creatures, reminiscent of those described in Ezekiel 1. When those living creatures 'give glory, honour and thanks' the elders 'fall down [...] and worship' (vv. 9-10). In other words, the living creatures fulfil a priestly role, leading the rest of heaven in worship.

New Testament scholar Richard Bauckham notes two very important details about this scene which ought to influence how we read it:[1]

John's Depiction of the Living Creatures is Unique & Specific

The heavenly throne-carriers of Ezekiel 1 were a popular image in John's day to depict the unceasing worship of heaven, and frequently appeared in apocalyptic literature. In every other instance, including Ezekiel, they appear as hybrids of many different creatures. But in John's vision each has a single likeness. Bauckham suggests that they are intended as representatives of four categories of living creatures: the lion for wild animals, the ox for domestic animals, the man for humanity and the eagle for the birds of the air.

> Revelation 4:6b-8 portrays the four living creatures as the central worshippers in creation, who, as heavenly representatives of all the animate creatures of the earth, unceasingly give to God the praise that all creation owes him.[2]

It is especially notable for us—who always seek out our own face in any photograph before that of others—that humanity is represented, but among fellow creatures. The human is not the chief worshipper. Rather, the group collectively leads the worship of heaven.

They Are All Waiting for Someone

As we continue into chapter five we discover there remains something incomplete about this scene of worship. The representatives of the heavenly court are waiting for someone to arrive, a fact which causes John some anguish. That someone turns out to be the 'Lamb, looking as if it

1 The following ideas are drawn from Bauckham, Richard, *Living With Other Creatures: Green Exegesis and Theology* (Milton Keynes: Paternoster, 2012), chapter 8.
2 *Ibid.*, 179.

had been slain'—the crucified, risen and ascended Jesus Christ—who takes his place at the centre of the throne (vv. 1-7). In this moment of coronation, the camera begins to pan back as new ripples of worship proceed outwards. The living creatures and the elders begin their ritual once more, but this time we see 100 million angels surrounding them in song, followed by 'every living creature in heaven and on earth and under the earth and on the sea, and all that is in them' (v. 13). Finally, the four living creatures can say, 'Amen' (v. 14).

Before the Lamb arrives, the priests of all created things are unceasing in their worship, but there is a sense in which their worship is impaired. It is only when the risen Son of God arrives, whose redeeming work has liberated all creation, that their worship is made complete and they are joined by literally everything that lives and breathes.

When we look for biblical models of worship, we are right to consider John's heavenly vision. But let us remember that to worship in this mould is to give 'praise and honour and glory and power' to 'him who sits on the throne and to the Lamb' (v. 13) together with our fellow creatures, with all living things, in a way that is only made possible through our risen saviour, Jesus Christ.

QUESTIONS FOR REFLECTION & DISCUSSION

1. Are there areas of your own life where you tend towards perfectionism? Why do you think that is?
2. Can you remember a time of corporate worship which was about as close to heavenly as you've experienced? What do you think made it so?
3. Are you surprised to discover that the four living creatures include humanity *alongside* representatives of all living things? What implications might this have for how you worship?
4. How could your church model its gathered worship if it learned from the scene in the heavenly courtroom?
5. Are there shortcomings in our earthly worship in general that we might have to simply accept until that 'great day' of the Lord?

Appendix
Service Plans

Introduction to the Service Plans

Sam Hargreaves, engageworship

The material that follows is designed so that you can run a three-week series on the themes of *Doxecology*. It gives you a short season in which you can introduce some of the new songs and thoroughly explore the idea of worshipping God by caring for his creation. In this way, your church will not only sing with understanding, but also be equipped to go out and live differently.

The material here is very much offered as a kind of buffet. Take whatever works for your context, adapt and tweak to suit your congregation, and ignore anything that just won't fit. There are downloadable PowerPoints, videos and printable sheets, but you could equally approach this in a low-tech way. Similarly, scripted prayers will be entirely natural for some churches, but will be new to other congregations so should be introduced with care. All age ideas are also presented, to give all generations an opportunity to participate together.

We realise that most churches can only absorb a limited number of new songs in a short period. For this reason, we'd suggest finding, say, three or four from the *Doxecology* album that you think will work best in your context, and use those repeatedly as congregational songs during the series. Other songs could be used via video for reflection, or performed by your band. You can then add more of the songs into your repertoire over the coming months. Where those *Doxecology* songs are included in the service plans they are indicated with a ***d***.

We have also recommended a number of songs and hymns from outside of the *Doxecology* album, some of which may already be sung by your church so would provide familiarity. Visit *www.doxecology.org/*

resources for hyperlinks to all the songs and hymns we suggest. Many churches now stream their services online. Do make use of the lyric videos to our songs for this purpose, and also feel free to use the PowerPoint files in these contexts.

Each sermon suggests using one chapter from this book as the basis. Preachers will most likely use this as a jumping-off point, and may well draw in ideas from other chapters or wider reading.

Outdoor Worship

This book equips us to worship our creator God in church buildings, so that we might be sent out to live in ways that honour his world. This is vital. But there is another piece to this puzzle. For the last few years I've been part of a group meeting in a local park twice a month, engaging in what we call Outdoor Worship.[1] This is not taking a PA system and a regular 'indoor' service out into the park, but instead allowing our gatherings to be shaped by the natural world.

Jesus says, 'consider the lilies [...] look at the birds'. What would it mean to take him at his word? To stand in the 'cathedral' of a forest, or be led by 'still waters' and 'green pastures', or experience the mighty mountains? To discuss with people of all ages how a snail's pace, or the wind's unseen power, or a seed buried in the ground speaks to us of the nature of God? Elizabeth Barrett Browning wrote:

> Earth's crammed with heaven,
> And every common bush afire with God
> But only he who sees, takes off his shoes...[2]

Stepping outside the doors of our churches and homes gives God an opportunity to open our eyes to his glory in the world around us. As we allow God to speak to us through nature, it will also shape our attitudes towards the planet. Just as no healthy Christian would trash their church building, every outdoor worshipper has a new-found respect for treading lightly on the earth.

1 http://www.parkchurchluton.com

2 From the poem, *Aurora Leigh*.

My challenge to you is, alongside running these three 'indoor' services, can you find a way to take your congregation outdoors? This could be a gentle walk guided by a local nature expert, or an all age session in the local woods (Forest Schools have a lot to teach us here), or a bird-spotting trip, or even simply twenty minutes of engaging with God in the church grounds or someone's garden.

We have shared a host of other road-tested ideas on our website, *https://engageworship.org/outdoor* and in our book *Outdoor Worship*. We also recommend the following books: *Outdoor Church* by Sally Welch and *Forest Church* by Bruce Stanley. Most importantly—be informed by the nature enthusiasts you have in your congregation, and allow your expression of outdoor worship to be shaped by where you find yourselves.

Service 1: The Beauty of Creation

Opening Prayer (based on Psalm 19)

Download: PowerPoint

LDR: The heavens declare the glory of God;
ALL: the skies proclaim the work of his hands.
Creation speaks without words,
announcing God's glory across the world.
We join with nature's song,
celebrating our creator God.

We have come to hear your word;
refresh our souls, make us wise, bring us joy.
Reveal our hidden faults,
cleanse us and restore us.
May the words of our mouths
and the thoughts of our hearts
be pleasing in your sight,
our Rock and our Redeemer.

Intro Video: Heaven's Voice Brings the Dawn

Download: Video

This video is an ideal introduction to the series and today's themes. It features the lyrics of the song, plus a wide range of creation imagery.

Opening Songs

God of Immeasurable Might - Andy Clark ***d***
Let All Creation Sing - Paul Zach & Andy Zipf ***d***
Indescribable - Laura Story, Jesse Reeves

Opening Hymns

All Creatures of Our God and King - W. H. Draper
Sing of the God who spoke - Martin Leckebusch

All Age: Picturing Creation

The week before, invite everyone in the congregation to send in photos of their favourite parts of God's creation. Combine these into a PowerPoint or video, or print them out as a gallery. You could also ask children to share verbally their favourite places in creation, and what they love about those places. The aim of this is simply to open up the theme and make it personal to your congregation.

All Age: Genesis 1 Rhyme Reading

Download: PowerPoint

Find a good reader to perform the 'verses'. To make this interactive, encourage everyone to join in the parts in bold. In an all age setting we would encourage people to shout the parts in capitals at the top of their voices (except the last one which you can whisper!), and to make up an action to reflect those words.

Rewind, back to the beginning,
no birds tweeting, no earth spinning.
Formless, nothing, 'til the day
God's Word and Spirit combined to say:

'LIGHT!'
And there was light.
It was a good light,
it was from God.

Somehow there was water, but it had no limits,
so God had to set some boundaries within it.
Once evening and morning had sailed on by
he divided heaven and earth with the cry:

'SKY!'
And there was sky.
It was a good sky,
it was from God.

Then God reached out his creative hand
to pull back the sea, revealing land.
He wanted to see diverse vegetation
food and colour for every generation:

'PLANTS!'
And there were plants.
They were good plants,
they were from God.

Now God wanted rhythms, days and nights,
seasons and patterns, shadows and lights.
So he set the stars and the moon in place
and he called with joy and delight on his face:

'SUN!'
And there was a sun.
It was a good sun,
it was from God.

God looked at the waters and looked at the sky,
he imagined sea creatures and things that fly,
all shades of colour, both huge and small,
and each appeared as he smiled and called:

'FISH AND BIRDS!'
And there were fish and birds.
They were good fish and good birds,
they were from God.

As he turned to land, God saw in his mind
creatures and critters of every kind,
tame and friendly, wild and wondrous,
at his voice there appeared in abundance:

'ANIMALS!'
And there were animals.
They were good animals,
they were from God.

The Trinity said, 'We need people like us,
male and female, united in love,
reflecting our nature, caring for earth,'
so with just one word God brought to birth:

'HUMANS!'
And there were humans.
They were good humans,
they were from God.

All God made, it was very, very good.
There were trees for shelter and plants for food.
The gift of creation with enough to share,
God blessed that day, and with a whisper declared:

'Rest.'
And there was rest.
It was a very good rest,
it was from God.

Bible Readings: Genesis 1, Psalm 148

Sermon: Worship With All Creation
(base this on Chapter 3)

Response: Creation Expression of Faith
Download: PowerPoint

This text is quite dense and asks people to make bold claims about what they believe, so you may wish to allow people a few minutes to read it through before you declare it together.

We believe in God the creator,
Jesus, the Word of creation,
the Holy Spirit, the breath of life.

We believe in the God who made all things good,
providing for and giving dignity to all he made,
holding all things together by his grace and love.

We believe that creation demonstrates God's glory,
revealing his invisible qualities,
his eternal power and divine nature.

We believe that the universe praises God,
honouring its creator and sustainer
with an endless, wordless symphony, to which we add our song.

We believe we are called to take responsibility for creation,
to be image-bearers and care-takers,
partnering creatively with God, nature and one another.

We believe that our selfishness has spoiled creation,
that sin has cosmic and worldwide consequences,
that creation groans to be restored.

We believe that on the cross
God was reconciling the world to himself,
and he will restore all things in heaven and on earth under Christ.

We believe that we are citizens of this renewed creation,
co-heirs with Christ and co-workers in the Spirit,
whose labours will echo into eternity.

We believe in God the creator,
that he has not given up on his creation,
and he has not given up on us.
Amen.

Response Song and Hymn

Nature Shines With Beauty - Chris Juby ***d***
For the Beauty of the Earth - F. S. Pierpoint

Blessing Prayer (adapted from Matthew 6:25-33)

The God who feeds the birds of the air,
will provide for your daily bread.
The God who clothes the flowers of the field
will meet all your needs.
The God of an infinite universe
sees you, loves you, calls you
to cast your worries on him
and seek first his kingdom on earth,
as it is in heaven.
Amen.

For downloads of items in the service, visit www.doxecology.org/resources

Service 2: The Cry of Creation

Opening Prayer (based on Psalm 24)

Download: PowerPoint

LDR: The earth is the Lord's,
ALL: and everything in it.
The world belongs to God.
every living thing is his.
God created it on the seas
and established it on the waters.

We have come today to meet with you, God.
But who may stand in your holy presence?
Clean our hands, purify our hearts,
that we might seek you and know your blessing.
Lift up our heads, open the gates,
as we welcome you here, King of Glory.

Opening Songs

From Life's Beginning (Let Praise Resound) - Marcus Pagnam
Let the Earth Find Rest - Chris Juby ***d***
Rejoice in All Your Works (Psalm 104) - Wendell Kimbrough

Opening Hymns

Great Is Thy Faithfulness - Thomas O. Chisholm
God, Creation Comes From You - Michael Baughen

Lament Video: Hear the Song of our Lament

Download: Video

This video of a song by Keiko Ying introduces some of the challenging themes of this week, around our misuse and mismanagement of God's world. It offers an opportunity to lament and seek God's forgiveness asking, 'Have mercy'.

All Age: Focus on Litter

Ask families to do a litter pick in a local park, woods or other outdoor space before the service, and then to come ready to talk about what they found. You could make gloves, litter-pickers and rubbish bags available, and ask families to take pictures of the litter they collect. Ask them to consider: Why do they think people drop litter? How did the litter make them feel? How do we think God feels about us dropping litter all over his world?

This could be a way of opening up a wider conversation about the way we manage our waste—plastic pollution, recycling, carbon emissions, oil spills and so on. You could show how different animals, habitats and people across the world are impacted by the ways we dispose of our rubbish.

All Age: Video Intro to Climate Change

https://operationnoah.org/resources/salote

This animated video from Operation Noah is a great way to introduce the issue of climate crisis, accessible by children and adults alike. It shows the immediate human impact of carbon emissions on people today. The website offers further printable resources for children.

Bible Readings: Ezekiel 37:1-14, Romans 8:18-25

Sermon: Confession for the Climate

(base this on Chapter 6)

Response Songs:

If the Fields are Parched - Chris Juby ***d***
Where Are You in the Storm? - Sam Hargeaves ***d***

Confession Prayer

Download: PowerPoint

> God who gives freedom,
> God who gives choices,
> each day we can choose how we treat your creation:

Thoughtlessly, or with a gardener's attention.
Carelessly, or with a shepherd's protection.
Selfishly, or with creative generosity.

We confess that we have fallen short
in the choices we have made
and the ways we've used our freedom.
We admit that we have not seen the world through your eyes,
and have not honoured you
in the ways we have treated your planet.

We believe you are a God of grace and transformation.
We trust you will forgive our mistakes,
restore your image in us,
and fill us with your Spirit to live differently.

Change our hearts, change our actions,
change attitudes and systems,
that we may glorify you
and restore your planet,
for the good of all creation.

In Jesus' name we pray,
Amen.

Receiving Forgiveness

We suggest you sing the song 'Why Are You Downcast' (Marcus Pagnam) as a way of being reminded of God's forgiveness and his enduring love.

Take-Home Cards: Living Differently

Download: Printable Sheets

These cards contain 10 practical ideas for simple ways to begin to live out a life that honours God's creation.

Blessing Prayer (adapted from Romans 8:18-24)

As creation waits in eager expectation
to be liberated from its bondage to decay
and brought into the freedom and glory of the children of God,
so may we, who have the firstfruits of the Spirit,
trust in the hope of God's saving power for us,
and for his whole creation.

Amen.

For downloads of items in the service, visit www.doxecology.org/resources

Service 3: The Hope of Creation

Opening Prayer (based on Isaiah 35)

Download: PowerPoint

LDR: In the wilderness of our broken world
ALL: we come to you for streams in the desert.
Strengthen our feeble hands,
steady the knees that give way;
say to those with fearful hearts,
'Be strong, do not fear, your God will come.'

Open our eyes, open our ears,
to know your promise of creation restored.
Lead us on your highway of holiness,
to walk with you, bringing life to your world.
We trust your promise that sorrow is temporary,
gladness and joy will be our eternal song.

Opening Songs

You Saw That It Was Good - Alex & Tim Fergusson ***d***
Look Up To the Skies - Judy Gresham
Creation Sings the Father's Song - Stuart Townend, Keith & Kristyn Getty

Opening Hymns

O Lord My God (How Great Thou Art) - Stuart K. Hine
God In Such Love For Us - Fred Pratt Green

Reflective Video: God the Word of Life (Great Day)

Download: Video

This song explores the tensions of what God promises to do on that 'great day' with the current reality that 'still, the earth groans'.

All Age: Planting Seeds Activity

Give everyone a cardboard plant pot (these are biodegradable and cheap to buy in bulk), some soil and some seeds, and a pen. Read John 12:24-25, and talk about Jesus' image of the seed having to go into the ground and 'dying' in order to be reborn. There is hope for our planet even beyond apparent 'death' - God works with us to bring resurrection.

This doesn't mean we can sit back and do nothing—we have a responsibility to care for the plant, to give it access to light and to water it. Ask people to reflect on what God is asking them to do to care for his planet, and write these things on their plant pot. Then encourage them to take their pots home, care for them, and whenever they see their pot to pray for creation and be reminded of the part they play in restoring it.

All Age: All The Broken And Dislocated Pieces

The Message paraphrase of Colossians 1:19-20 says about Jesus: 'So spacious is he, so roomy, that everything of God finds its proper place in him without crowding. Not only that, but all the broken and dislocated pieces of the universe—people and things, animals and atoms—get properly fixed and fit together in vibrant harmonies, all because of his death, his blood that poured down from the Cross.'

Find a pile of magazines with images of creation in them, and ask a group to tear these pictures out. As they are doing so, read out the verses above, and talk about how God's world is broken and dislocated, torn and crumpled like our magazine pictures. Then produce a large cross formed of wood or paper, and invite the group to take their torn images and stick them to it. Reflect on how Jesus' cross restores God's broken creation.

Bible Readings: Colossians 1:15-23, Revelation 22:1-5

Sermon: The Cross and Creation

(base this on Chapter 9)

Intercession Prayer (Based on Revelation 21:1-5, 22:1-5)

Download: PowerPoint

Creator God,
we believe the promise of your word,
that heaven and earth will be renewed.
As we look at the planet you have made,
we see pollution and destruction,
carelessness and mismanagement.
Yet we believe you bring life from death,
and that you want to partner with us
in restoring your creation.

Your words are trustworthy and true:
ALL: Help us, God, to work with you.
Your word says earth will be renewed:
ALL: Help us, God, to work with you.

We pray for governments and businesses,
the powerful and the influencers,
that their priorities would change
and the good of all creation would come before greed and self-interest.
May the resources you have given be used responsibly,
shared with equity, and processed sustainably.
Make us mindful of every creature, plant and habitat,
each a valued part of your creation;
make us conscious of every nation, people group and generation,
each made in your image.

Your words are trustworthy and true:
ALL: Help us, God, to work with you.
Your word says earth will be renewed:
ALL: Help us, God, to work with you.

We pray for those who work in nature,
for farmers, gardeners and rangers,
and every hand that seeks to shape and protect your world.
Use the gifts and passions of ordinary people
to make a difference.
And we pray for ourselves,
that our spending power, our voices and our everyday actions
would be empowered by your Spirit
to contribute to the healing of your planet.

Your words are trustworthy and true:
ALL: Help us, God, to work with you.
Your word says earth will be renewed:
ALL: Help us, God, to work with you.

We look forward to the day
when the river of life will flow as clear as crystal.
We choose to work for the day
when the tree of life will bear fruit
and its leaves will be for the healing of the nations.
We choose to live now
in anticipation of eternity
on a renewed earth,
creation no longer cursed,
with you, God, at the centre of it all.

Your words are trustworthy and true:
ALL: Help us, God, to work with you.
Your word says earth will be renewed:
ALL: Help us, God, to work with you.
Amen.

Holy Communion

https://operationnoah.org/resources/a-creation-communion

This would be a good week to celebrate Holy Communion as part of your series. We realise that patterns around the Lord's Table are different for each denomination and church, but you may find it helpful to incorporate aspects of Sylvia Walker's *A Creation Communion*.

Response and Sending Songs

We are the Tenants of the King - Joel Payne ***d***
God the Maker of the Heavens - Sam Hargreaves ***d***
So Will I (100 Billion X) - Joel Houston, Benjamin Hastings, Michael Fatkin

Blessing Prayer (adapted from Numbers 6:24-26)

The Lord bless his world and keep it,
guard it and sustain it,
nurture it and restore it,
make his face shine upon it
and give it peace.
Amen.

For downloads of items in the service, visit www.doxecology.org/resources